SUNFLOWERS

SUNFLOWERS

by Cynthia Overbeck

Photographs by Susumu Kanozawa

A Lerner Natural Science Book

Lerner Publications Company ▪ Minneapolis

Sylvia A. Johnson, Series Editor

Translation by Joe and Hiroko McDermott

Additional research by Jane Dallinger

The publisher wishes to thank Thomas Morley,
Professor of Botany, University of Minnesota,
for his assistance in the preparation of this book.

LIBRARY OF CONGRESS CATALOGING IN PUBLICATION DATA

Overbeck, Cynthia.
  Sunflowers.

  (A Lerner natural science book)
  Adapted from Observing the sunflower, by M. Shirako,
originally published under title: Himawari no kansatsu.
  Includes index.
  Summary: Text and photographs describe the growth
of a sunflower from a seed to a full-grown plant.
  1. Sunflowers—Juvenile literature. [1. Sunflowers]
I. Kanōzawa, Susumu, 1942- . II. Shirako, Morizō.
Himawari no kansatsu. English. III. Title. IV. Series:
Lerner natural science book.

QK495.C74092   583′.55   80-27797
ISBN 0-8225-1457-5

This edition first published 1981 by Lerner Publications Company.
Revised text copyright © 1981 by Lerner Publications Company.
Photographs copyright © 1973 by Susumu Kanozawa.
Adapted from OBSERVING THE SUNFLOWER copyright © 1973
by Morizō Shirako. English language rights arranged by
Japan UNI Agency, Inc. for Akane Shobo Publishers, Tokyo.

International Standard Book Number: 0-8225-1457-5
Library of Congress Catalog Card Number: 80-27797

1 2 3 4 5 6 7 8 9 10 90 89 88 87 86 85 84 83 82 81

One of the prettiest sights of summer is a field of golden sunflowers swaying on top of their tall stems. These giant flowers grow in many parts of the United States, as well as in Europe, Russia, and Japan. Many people grow sunflowers in their gardens. Sunflower plants also grow wild, adding color to empty lots and railroad yards. In many countries, farmers plant large crops of sunflowers for harvest. The seeds of the sunflower are good to eat, and the oil that is pressed from them has many uses.

There are over 220,000 kinds of flowering plants, and they are divided into many different families. Sunflowers are members of the family Compositae. The plants in this family are made in a special way. Each flower head looks like a single flower but is really made up of many tiny flowers growing close together. This kind of flower is called a **composite** flower.

Composite flowers like the sunflower grow in the same basic way that all flowering plants grow. Although flowering plants can have different parts and different ways of reproducing, they all have one thing in common. The life story of each begins and ends with a seed.

Plant seeds come in all sizes. They can be so small as to be almost invisible without a microscope, or they can be as big as a coconut. The seed of the sunflower is small—about a half inch (1.2 cm) long. On the outside is a hard striped covering. This protects the soft, grayish seed inside. The seed itself contains the parts needed to produce a new plant. It also contains two tiny seed leaves, or **cotyledons**. The rest of the seed is made up of food that the cotyledons will use when the seed is ready to grow into a plant.

A seed needs warmth, water, and air in order to grow. This is why the seeds of sunflowers and other plants sprout, or begin to grow, in the springtime. In spring, the ground and the air warm up, and the soil receives plenty of water from spring rains and melting snow. As soon as the seed is planted in the soil, the amazing process of **germination**, or sprouting, begins.

Under the ground, the water in the soil begins to soften the hard outer covering. Inside, the seed is getting ready to sprout. The pictures on the opposite page show what happens. About three days after planting, a tiny white root pushes through the seed covering. As this root grows downward, a stem begins to grow upward. On about the seventh day after planting, the stem breaks through the ground and into the air. By this time the cotyledons, or seed leaves, have grown too large to be kept inside by the outer covering. As these leaves open, the covering splits and falls off (above). The new sunflower plant has begun to grow.

Like all flowering plants, the new sunflower plant will have four main parts. The first three are the **vegetative** parts of the plant. These are the roots, stems, and leaves. The fourth part will be the flowers and seeds, or **reproductive** parts.

The root is the first part of the plant to develop. As the plant grows, many smaller roots branch off the main root. They form a network under the ground. These roots hold the sunflower plant firmly in the soil. They also take in water and minerals from deep in the soil and pass them to the upper parts of the plant.

The water and minerals move to the top of the sunflower through the stem. Bundles of very tiny tubes within the stem carry water in much the same way that pipes do.

This sunflower stem was put into red ink. After the stem absorbed the ink, it was cut in half lengthwise and across. The enlarged picture on the left shows how the ink has moved through tiny tubes up the stem. The small picture shows the end of the stem. The red dots are the ends of the tubes.

11

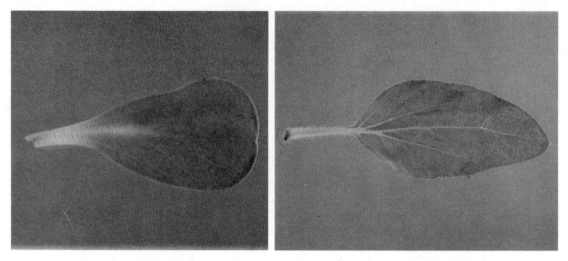

A cotyledon   A true leaf

As the little sunflower plant continues to grow, the two cotyledons get bigger. These cotyledons are not true leaves, but special thick leaves that contain food from the seed. They supply the food to the rest of the **seedling**, or young plant, during the early stages of growth.

Soon, the first set of true leaves appears between the two cotyledons. These leaves are thinner than the cotyledons and a different shape. Along with the roots, the true leaves will soon take over the job of making food for the whole plant.

To make food, a leaf uses water and minerals carried from the roots. It also uses air and sunlight. The leaf takes in light energy from the sun. At the same time, carbon dioxide gas and water from the air enter the leaf through many holes, too tiny to see, on the leaf's surface. Meanwhile, water and

12

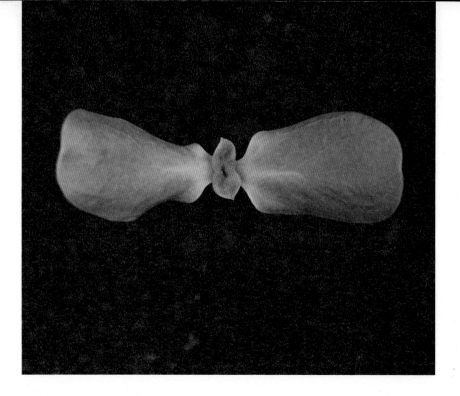

minerals from the soil are also entering the leaf through the stem. The sun's energy combines this mixture of gas, water, and minerals to make a kind of sugar that is changed into food for the plant. The plant uses the food to help it grow and to repair itself. This process of making food is called **photosynthesis**.

The leaf is specially made to do the important job of photosynthesis. A thin stem joins the leaf to the plant's main stem. The leaf stem carries water and food to and from the leaf. The little veins on the leaf itself carry water throughout the leaf. The veins also serve as a kind of frame to hold the leaf's surface open to the sun. The many tiny holes on the surface let water and gases pass in and out of the leaf.

As the sunflower plant grows, more and more true leaves grow out of its main stem. The new leaves are arranged on the stem so that they receive as much sunlight as possible. The leaves grow in pairs, and each new pair of leaves grows at right angles across the pair below it. This lets the sunlight reach the surface of all the leaves.

Now that the sunflower plant has its true leaves, it can make food for itself through photosynthesis. The plant no longer needs the food stored in the cotyledons. So the cotyledons droop and wither. Soon they will fall off. In the picture on the right, the arrows point to the cotyledons, which are about to drop off.

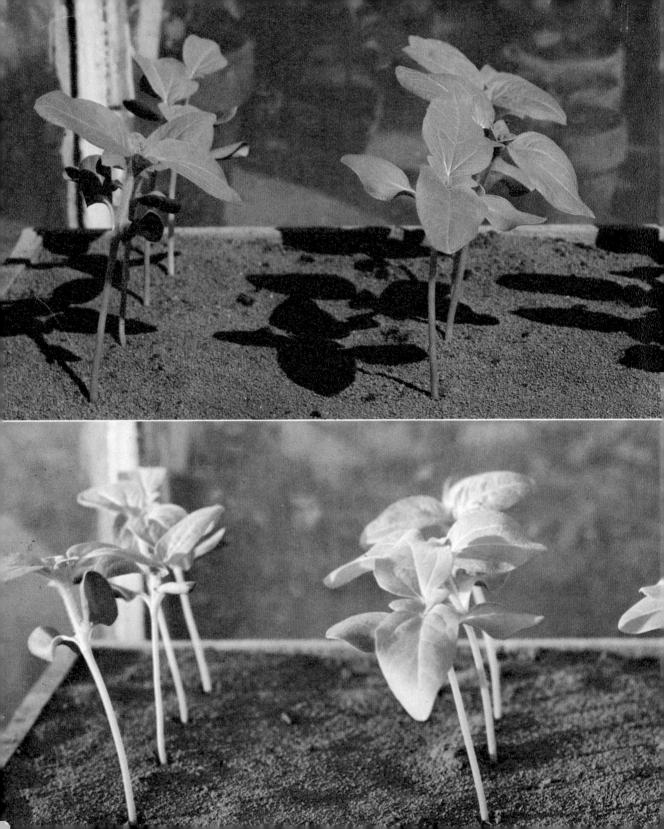

Sunflower seedlings need as much of the sun's energy as they can capture. For this reason, they actually lean toward the sun. Throughout the day, as the sun's position in the sky changes, the little plants follow the sun's light. The seedlings in the picture show this happening. At 10:00 AM, the seedlings have turned their heads east toward the morning sun. By 5:00 PM in the evening, the same seedlings are leaning west, toward the setting sun. Just before sunrise on the next day, they will still be facing west. But in a half hour they will have turned toward the east to face the rising sun. This bending toward the light is called **phototropism**. As the sunflower plant grows, it will continue to move with the sun until it has almost finished flowering.

17

Once the sunflower seedling begins to develop true leaves, it grows quickly. In about two months' time, a typical plant is 7.5 feet (2.25 meters) tall. Its main stem is thick and strong, and its leaves are broad. Smaller stems begin to branch off the main stem. Toward the top of the plant, **buds** appear where the leaves join the main stem. Some of these buds will grow to be branches; some will be other leaves. Soon, other buds grow at the ends of the branches. And at the very top of the stem, a large bud begins to form. This bud and the buds at the branch ends are the ones that will become flowers.

This bud is a ball of tightly packed flower petals. It is protected by overlapping rows of pointed green **bracts**. The bracts are curled tightly around the unopened flower. When the flower is ready to open, the bracts open first.

Slowly the bud opens to show the bright yellow petals of the sunflower. One by one the petals rise straight up; then they open out flat. This blooming process is quick. It takes only about a day and a half.

Once it is in bloom, the head of a sunflower may be as big as 2 feet (60 cm) across. The plant itself grows up to 18 feet (5.4 meters) tall. Its roots, which may be 9 feet (2.7 meters) long, take water from deep in the soil. Its huge leaves soak up the energy of the hot summer sun. The sunflower plant is strong and hardy.

By now the plant is about three months old. Up until this time, most of its energy has gone into its vegetative parts— roots, stem, and leaves. Now, the growth begins in the plant's reproductive parts—the flowers. Producing flowers is this huge plant's most important job. For it is the flowers that produce seeds, which in turn will produce new sunflower

plants. Within this large and beautiful flower, a complicated process of reproduction begins to take place.

The open sunflower looks like one huge flower, with a large dark center surrounded by yellow petals. But, like all members of the family Compositae, a single sunflower head is really a cluster of many tiny flowers growing together. The center of a large sunflower is made up of more than 2,000 tiny, tube-like flowers. These are called **disk florets**. The giant yellow petals around the outside of the sunflower head are called **ray florets**. The disk florets grow close together on the flat center, or **disk**, of the sunflower. The ray florets are arranged around the outer edge. The green bracts that once protected the bud now hold up the disk.

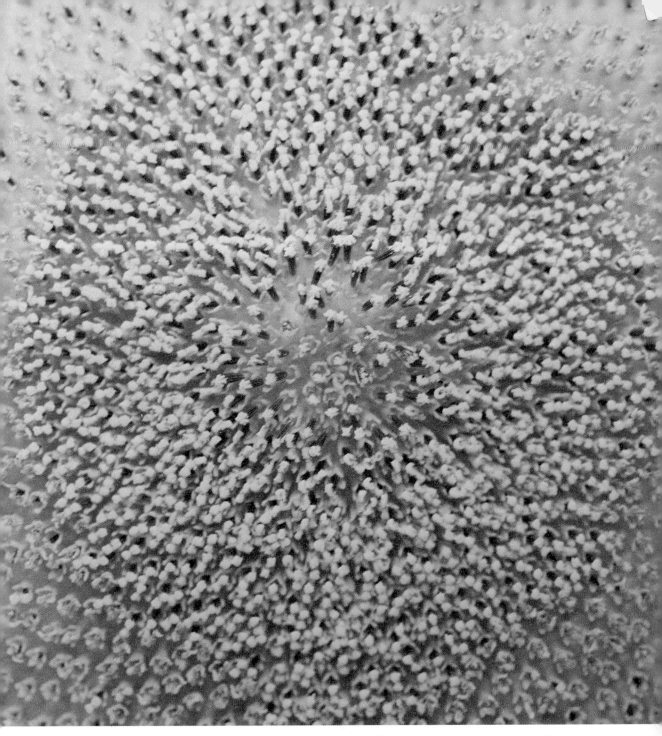

This close-up picture of the sunflower's center shows the many tiny disk florets.

Each tiny disk floret is a complete flower in itself. Each blooms separately. The ones nearest the outside edge of the disk are the first to open their five pointed yellow petals. Then, one by one, the others begin to open their petals.

The picture on the left, above, shows a sunflower head on which only the florets around the edges are in bloom. The rounded yellow knobs are unopened florets. When all of these have opened, the sunflower will look like the picture on the right. The picture on the opposite page shows the florets magnified many times. The ones at the top are open. The others with the round tops still have not bloomed.

28

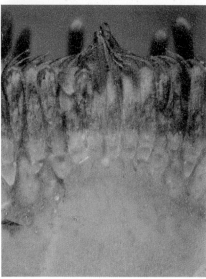

This sunflower head has been cut in half to show how the disk florets are arranged on the disk. The florets on the outside edges are already in bloom.

Each sunflower floret is made up of several parts that work together to produce a single seed. A floret has both male and female parts. In the center of the floret is the female part—the **pistil.** At its base is a kind of hollow bag called the **ovary.** Within the ovary is a tiny **ovule** containing an egg cell that will grow into a seed. A **style,** or small stalk, grows out of the ovary. At its top is the **stigma**—a knob that will later open up into two curly little "arms" to receive pollen.

The male part of the floret is called the **stamen.** Five stamens grow around one pistil. Each stamen is made up of one **filament** and one **anther.** The filament is a thread-like stalk. At its top is a slender black anther, which is filled with yellow **pollen.** Pollen is the powdery "flower dust" that contains male sperm cells.

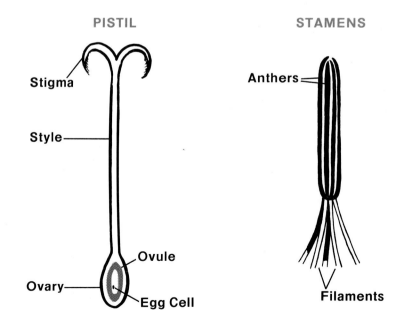

PISTIL   STAMENS

Stigma

Style

Ovule

Ovary

Egg Cell

Anthers

Filaments

This photo shows a disk floret in all its stages of growth. From left to right, it is: 1) unopened; 2) getting ready to bloom; 3) in bloom, with the black stamens rising above the petals; 4) ready to receive pollen, with its stigma open; 5) fertilized, with a seed growing in the ovary.

In order for a seed to grow in the ovary, a sperm cell from the anthers must unite with, or **fertilize,** an egg cell in the ovule. But first, pollen containing the sperm must reach the stigma. The transfer of pollen to a stigma is called **pollination.**

Flowering plants are pollinated in two different ways. The stigma of a flower may receive pollen from anthers on the same flower or from anthers on a different flower of the same plant. This process is called **self-pollination.** When the pollen comes from flowers of a completely different plant, the process is called **cross-pollination.** Once the pollen has landed on the stigma, fertilization can take place Some kinds of sunflowers that have been specially developed as crops are fertilized through self-pollination. But in their

The picture on the opposite page shows grains of pollen, magnified many times. The smaller picture shows the pollen-covered pistil surrounded by the black anthers of the stamens.

FLORET CUT IN HALF

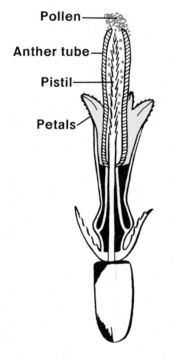

Pollen

Anther tube

Pistil

Petals

natural state, sunflowers usually are not fertilized by sperm from their own pollen. Instead they are fertilized by sperm they receive through cross-pollination from another sunflower plant.

Each part of the sunflower's pistil and stamen has a special part to play in the complicated process of pollination and fertilization. In each floret, the male stamens grow closely around the female pistil. The black anthers form a kind of tube. When the yellow petals of the floret open, they reveal the anther tube with the pistil inside. As the pistil grows inside the tube, the anthers drop their pollen on it. At this point, the two arms of the stigma are still tightly closed. As the pistil grows with the closed stigma on its tip, it pushes the sticky yellow pollen up and out the end of the anther tube.

For cross-pollination to take place, this pollen must somehow reach the pistils of another sunflower plant. Now the plant needs help from the insect world. The florets make **nectar**, a sweet, sticky liquid that attracts insects. Bees, wasps, and butterflies visit the sunflower in order to eat this nectar. The bright outer petals—the ray florets—of the sunflower attract these insects to the flower and provide a kind of landing platform for them. The insects land on the ray florets and begin crawling over the center of the sunflower.

As the insects move along, eating nectar, the sticky pollen on top of the many florets rubs off on their legs and bodies. When the insects have eaten as much nectar as they can find, they fly off to another sunflower plant. Then, as they crawl over this next flower, some of the pollen from the previous plant rubs off onto this flower's pistils.

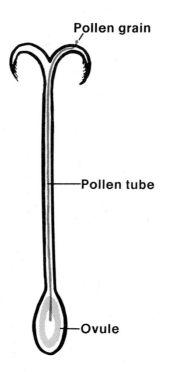

Pollen grain

Pollen tube

Ovule

By this time, the stigmas on the tops of the pistils have developed to the stage where they are ready to receive pollen. Their two arms have opened up and are spread wide. When pollen falls on an open stigma, the sunflower floret is pollinated.

The next step in the process of making a seed is fertilization. For this to happen, a sperm cell from the pollen must get into the ovary. A grain of pollen splits open and sends a long **pollen tube** down the style and into the ovary. A tiny sperm cell drops down through the tube. It comes together with an egg cell in the ovule, and the egg is fertilized. When this happens, a seed begins to grow in the ovary.

This sunflower has been pollinated and fertilized. Now it has begun to grow seeds that will produce new sunflower plants.

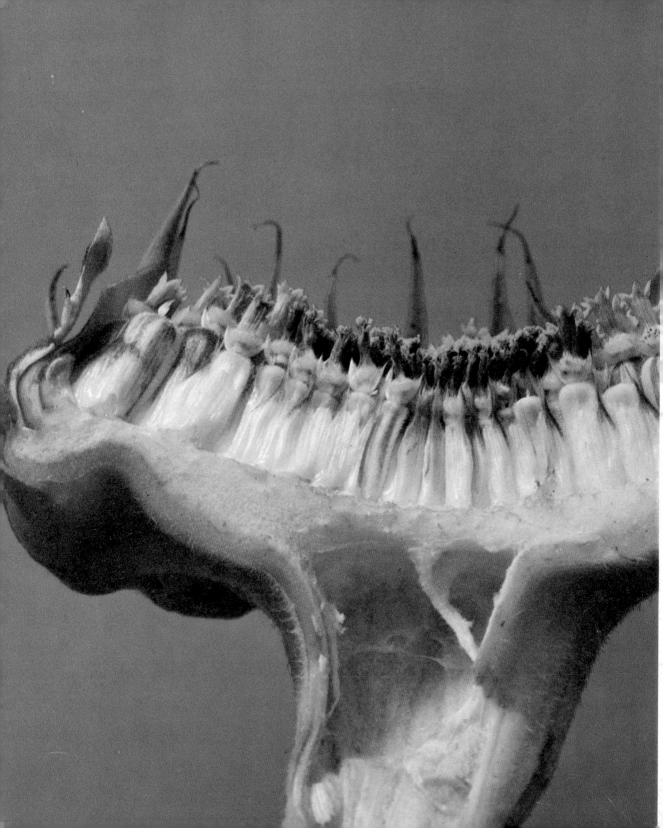

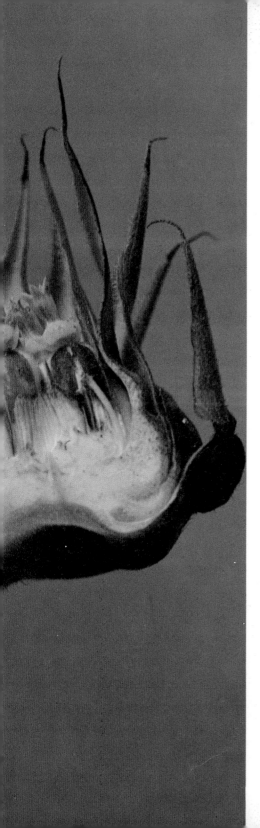

Once all the seeds within the sunflower florets are growing, the main job of the flower is finished. The flower has really lived only to produce seeds. Now that the yellow ray florets are no longer needed to attract insects, they wither and curl up. The yellow disk florets stop making nectar and pollen. They, too, wither and turn dark.

As summer comes to an end, the sunflower plant puts all its energy into making food to help the seeds to grow. Within the ovary of each floret, the seed grows bigger and bigger. Each seed grows straight up with its pointed end attached to the broad disk of the sunflower head. As this cutaway picture shows, the seeds near the outside of the disk develop first, just as the florets in that part of the flower were the first to open.

By fall, all the seeds have grown to their full size. In a large sunflower, there may be as many as 2,000 of them. Now each looks just like the seed that was originally planted. Each has a hard, striped covering that protects the seed within. The joints that hold each seed to the disk dry out, and one by one, the seeds fall to the ground.

Once the seeds have matured and fallen to the ground, the plant's job is done. The disk becomes an empty shell, and the stalk and all the leaves wither and die.

If the sunflowers were planted as a crop, the seeds are harvested by farmers in the fall. Oil is pressed from the seeds of some kinds of sunflowers. This oil is used for cooking or as a base for paints and soaps. The part of the seed that is left after pressing is fed to farm animals. The dry seed coverings can be made into logs and used for fuel. Seeds harvested from other kinds of sunflowers are used for human food and for bird seed.

Some sunflower seeds are kept to be planted next spring. When the earth becomes warm and the spring rains fall, the seeds will sprout. Then the cycle of growth and reproduction will begin again.

GLOSSARY

anther—the part of a flower's stamen that contains pollen

bracts (BRAKTS)—small leaves that grow around a bud and help to protect it.

bud—a small swelling on a plant from which a leaf, stem, or flower develops

composite flower—a flower whose head is made up of many small flowers. Composite flowers are members of the family Compositae.

cotyledon (kaht-'l-EED-un)—a seed leaf

cross-pollination—the depositing of pollen from one plant onto the stigma of another plant

disk—the flat center of a sunflower

disk florets—tiny, tube-like flowers that grow in the center of the sunflower

fertilization—the uniting of a male sperm cell and a female egg cell to produce a seed

filament—the stalk of a stamen

germination—the sprouting of a seed

nectar—a sweet liquid produced by flowers to attract insects

ovary—the part of the pistil in which a seed grows

ovule (OH-vyool)—the tiny structure in the pistil that grows into a seed

photosynthesis (fot-uh-SIN-thuh-sis)—the process that plants use to make food

phototropism (foh-TAT-reh-piz'm)—a bending in response to light

pistil (PIS-tuhl)—the seed-producing part of a flower

pollen (PAHL-ehn)—a yellow, powdery substance containing sperm cells that come together with the ovule in a flower to make a seed

pollen tube—a tiny tube that carries sperm cells from a pollen grain into the ovary of a flower

pollination—the process by which pollen comes together with the stigma of a flower

ray florets—the yellow petals that grow around the outside edge of the sunflower

reproductive parts—the stamens, pistils, fruits, and seeds of a flowering plant

seedling—a young plant grown from a seed

self-pollination—the depositing of pollen from a flower onto its own stigma or onto the stigma of another flower on the same plant

stamen (STAY-mehn)—the pollen-producing part of a flower

stigma—the part of the pistil that receives pollen

style (STILE)—the narrow part of the pistil that supports the stigma

vegetative parts—the roots, stems, and leaves of a flowering plant

INDEX